Lo e Bites

By
Demetria Keesee

About The Author

Demetria is a teacher, the Author of *Legs Wide Open* and contributing author of *Beauty for Ashes, Bruised but NOT Broken*. Demetria resides in Virginia. She attended Norfolk State University where she received her B.S. in Early Childhood Education Prek-3. Demetria is also a member of Delta Sigma Theta Sorority, Inc. When she's not writing, Demetria is doing a combination of the following: writing poems, prayer, binge reading books, working out, spending time with family and friends, dancing and listening to an eclectic assortment of music.

Follow her on Instagram and TikTok @deekeesee
For booking for speaking engagements email:
keeseespeaks@gmail.com

Foreword

by

Kristy Lyles

Love Bites is a book that was birthed out of a sincere burden for Christian singles to be encouraged during their wait for Godly marriage. Singleness can sometimes feel like a "season of punishment" when not viewed from the proper perspective, and Love Bites was written to, hopefully, transform the reader's possible "jaded" viewpoint on singleness by renewing their mind. Filled with an abundance of inspirational poems, quotes, scriptures, and sketches... Love Bites is an uplifting journey through God's Word on how to both love and wait God's way. With so many Christian singles beginning to question God's timing and doubt His plan for their romantic future, we need as many sources of Godly encouragement as possible...and Love Bites was written for such a time as this. Author Demetria Keesee pours out her heart for singles through her writing and, when received properly, this book can be an amazing tool to guide the reader in a greater dimension of faith, patience and, prayerfully, LOVE.

Dedication

The book is for Christian singles waiting for their
God-send.
Be encouraged, I pray these LOVE BITES speak to
your heart.
Stay in faith.

With love,
deekeesee

*Delight thyself also in the LORD: and he shall give the
desires of thine heart.* **Psalm 37:4 KJV**

Introduction

"Do not arouse or awaken love until it so desires".(Song of Solomon NIV)

Three times this scripture placed emphasis on not arousing love before it's time. But, why not? Is it some waiting game we have to enter in order to experience love in its fullest? I asked myself this question, often wondering why love sends this euphoric shock of arousal to the body. As love enters, it sends off these wavelengths of joy, sending chills and goosebumps down your spine.

I want all the smoke. Send it up and send it through like D'Angelo would say, lol. I want it to send me the chills, goosebumps, and butterflies—all the above. Yet, we are still reminded in scripture "do not arouse or awaken love until it's so desire" (Song of Solomon NIV). Why is that? I think I understand why.

Jumping into love prematurely, when you haven't developed a full understanding or foundation upon which to care for it, love it, embrace it, appreciate it and accept it before it's time, can do more damage to you than good. If this love is rushed too soon, we stop believing in it because of hurt and disappointment. We then make up in our mind that the love and marriage fairytale doesn't exist. But really, is that true? Not everyone's reality and experience of love is the same, yet deep down we all drift back into our childhood perception of what love is and what it could possibly be for us.

For some, love should have been the fairytale story of Cinderella and Prince Charming hoping that a love like theirs can be true for you. While we all may still be hoping for this for ourselves, over time the dream and thought of it finding us makes us tired of the wait. We no longer expect it to be true. We stop believing in love and the magic wrapped in it. But if you're like me, you still know it's out there waiting for you. What do you believe about love? Can dreams really come true?

I mean, why do we desire the fairytale? And if fairytales are not realistic, why are there so many stories written and displayed about it? Not to mention how some people like to project their love story all over social media. Makes you think, is that real or just a trend for new Instagram content? Scripture tells us in 1 John 4:18, "there is no fear in love, but perfect love drives out fear". This makes me wonder, just like in any romantic fairytale, what if true love's kiss does exist? I mean, why is that even so hard to believe? We should be able to believe in love and the possibility of it, yet if we are not careful we can fall into the *LOVE BITES* too soon.

My mother emphasized I should be careful in choosing who I love and who I decide to give my heart to. My dad told me to make sure he was right before I give myself away. If love is supposed to be this beautiful thing we all long to receive, there is still great emphasis to wait for love and not awaken love until it's time. Having these warnings made me ask, were the butterflies and this new arousal of love even a good sign? Why did my mother warn me and why was this mentioned more than once in the Bible? I didn't understand. I thought the butterflies were a good sign, but for some reason, if you are not wise or you have discernment, this butterfly feeling can arouse love too soon. And what makes it worse is when it's aroused by the wrong person.

Love is so powerful—that's why God created it, but if it is not placed and properly nourished in the right hands, it can hit you hard and bite you in the worst way. These are not the kind of 'love bites' God desires for you to experience. This is not to scare you away. For those who still believe in love, keep reading, because this is for you. The kind of *LOVE BITES* God wants to bring into your life will be abundant. These *LOVE BITES* are the kind of love and expectation God intends for you to have. You see God's love is pure, it's intentional, and it flows, but if this feeling of love is awakened too soon, it can cause some heartbreak.

I'm here to tell you God does not spend heartbreak. You truly cannot believe that He will send you a man of God to break your heart and make you cry over and over again. Why would our loving Father do that? Going back to what my mom warned me about, which made me hesitant and question if I even desired marriage or want to be in love in the first place, I decided to take a leap of faith and trust that who God has for me will feel just like these *LOVE BITES*.

I wrote this book in the hope that if I trust in God and knowing that He is not a man who lies, would mean that all my praying and expectation would not be in vain, because I put my trust in Him and He knows my heart. This book is to help you believe in love again and trust God first with your heart. Your *LOVE BITES* are not far from reach. Very soon one day you will be able to look into the love of your life's eyes and truly be fulfilled with a knowing that surely this is God's best for you.

These *LOVE BITES* are very possible to have. It's sad that some will never get to experience it, while others do, and some just can only pray and imagine. I know this may be a lot for some to take in, but if this sounds like you, and you have been feeling worried, concerned, or anxious about meeting "the one", allow these *LOVE BITES* to bring you peace of mind as you read through each poem and chapter to remind you love is for you.

I pray you receive the love that your heart desires. And when you do, I pray it will continue to give you a fulfilled love of these *LOVE BITES*. The kind of *LOVE BITES* that won't break your heart, but are there to stay. The kind of *LOVE BITES* that bring out the joy in you, and healing. The kind of

LOVE BITES that will make you smile on a regular day. These *LOVE BITES* that I share with you, I pray they bring you peace of mind and some rest, because who God has in store for you next, is way better than the one who left. These *LOVE BITES* are sweet and gentle to the heart, like a forehead kiss letting you know that these *LOVE BITES* are not far from where you are. It's very possible to have this. Believe in love again, these *LOVE BITES* exist. They are who you are.

If you are willing and ready, can I take you on a journey to love? A journey to finding love God's way? I prayed and asked God that if, and only if, there's a chance that this feeling of these *LOVE BITES* is true; that this is the feeling you have when you meet "the one", then let me first find it in Him. Until He sends "the one", allow these *LOVE BITES* to bring you peace, assurance, and trust that God is not a man who will lie. He will fulfill His promise. We all know getting hurt sucks, but that shouldn't stop you from taking a chance on someone who could make you extremely happy. Just in case you change your mind, wait on God: it's only a matter of time. Find peace in the wait with these *LOVE BITES*.

"Don't excite love, don't stir it up, until the time is ripe and you're ready." *(Song of Solomon 8: 4 NIV)*

Table of Contents

Table of Contents

Table of Contents

CHAPTER
1

♥

LETTER TO HIM

Letter To Him

I have been praying. Praying scriptures and writing these words to you. Are you really my love? Will my dreams ever come true? I don't want to fight my feelings, I know I'm hard to get to. Sometimes stubborn, but pure at heart, I pray you see me. I covered you in my prayers, God's got everything under control. My faith is in Him; I know He will give me the ability to see. I was able to look up because I sensed it was you for me.

What I Need

You are my provider; I am your peace.

Through trials and tests, you are all that I need.

A heart like David, wisdom like Samuel,

there really isn't anything you couldn't handle.

Faith like Paul, you're so quick on your feet.

When I'm tired or thirsty, you bring me something to eat.

Courageous like Joshua, creative like Noah.

These are the fruits of your labor, I see what you are

sowing.

Worker like Boaz, just like Abraham, established the

foundation by grace through God, not even knowing.

You set out on a mission like Joseph. You're like

Moses; you didn't sweat the pressure, you kept going.

What can I do for you, to show you my love is

FOREVER growing? How can I help you?

And if you ever ask how can you be the man for me?

By loving God FIRST, that is all that I need.

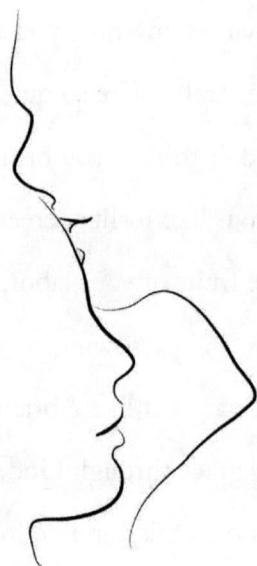

Thoughts Of You

You said this before, all of it is true.

These are the thoughts that I think of you.

This is how I want you to love me,

show me God through you.

Put Him first, love Him always,

then you can see my worth and what I do.

You will treat me with so much care.

Providing for me is a given, it's me you see, do you

dare?

Do you dare to go above and beyond for me?

Your actions are so sweet!

Tell me you love me, and it's me that you seek.

I Am Your Good Thing

I am your good thing, and you know it.
Whenever you see me you get this excited grin on
your face, as you draw near to me with your warm
embrace. You don't just tell me you love me, but you
always show me with your actions.

I am your good thing, and I'm glad you know it.
You're not just in love with the looks and shape of
me. You see into me. You love my mind, my
goodliness, my laugh, my energy. You get me. You
don't find me strange for thinking the way I do. You
always support and back up my creative thoughts.
That's dope, how we both vibe together.

You see how I am your good thing? I know you
knew it.
Seeing you is like seeing God in manifestation. We
are moved by each other. We pray together, stay
together, we are drawn towards each other. Our
innocence for each other is like the beautiful

laughter of children. You love me like a fat kid who loves cake. Mmmm, I think I want a taste, lol. I love how you cover me, you take my hand and say, "babe, let's pray." You are a positive, motivating force within my life.

I am your good thing, and you know it.
It says a man that finds a wife, finds a good thing.
I am the "thing", I am your "Good THING" and
I'm glad you know it.

ou Understand Me

You are the thunder to my lightning, the match to my flame.

I'm so glad you found me, I like the way you say my name.

Your voice is deep, you see pass my imperfections and yet you're still here, no hiding you just understand me.

I see passion and ambition, not easy to be threatened.

There's so much more in you, how could I forget?

Bold and courageous, your laughter is contagious.

You have the keys to my heart, my guard is now down.

I see the light within you; you hold the ROYAL CROWN.

Usher Me

Usher me into your heart.

Allow me to take a sit and enjoy this ride until death do us part.

Usher me

Usher me into my next level of thinking. Expand my mind, show me a new vision so I can spot the dart.

Usher me

Usher me until I go into a metamorphosis, change the way I do life, see life, a clear vision of a new start.

Usher me

Usher me out of my old habits so past thoughts vanish, and cleanse me from the inside out.

Usher me

Usher me with your love, allow me to feel your mind and emotions from a pure heart.

Usher me

Usher me with your peace and stability. Allow me to flow in the gifts of what God called me to be,

having certainty that you will be my help and
support system if I slip, or fail, or come up short.

Usher me

Usher me into a deep prayer, allow consecration to
take off to a new level deeper beyond where I
started.

Usher me

Usher me onto the stage, as I stand there boldly,
having full confidence and authority and belief in
myself. Help me to see this confidence in myself
that the Lord has given.

Usher me

Usher me with your patience, empowering me to
believe in myself and to keep going, no matter what.

Usher me

Usher me every day through your commitment to
love. Hold and cherish me until death do us part.

The Right Path

Obtain the vision; the provision will come next.

God's hands are over your case—that should bring you

some rest.

Stop looking for all the right answers,

it's okay—you will never be a mess.

God will renew you again, He only sees you as His

best.

Scriptures

LETTER TO HIM

Ephesians 5:25 NLT *"For husbands, this means you love your wives, just as Christ loved the church. He gave up his life for her."*

Genesis 2:24 NIV "That is why a man leaves his father and mother and is united to his wife, and they become one flesh".

Genesis 2:18 NIV "Then the LORD God said, "It is not good that the man should be alone; I will make him a helper fit for him."

CHAPTER 2

LETTER TO HER

Letter To Her

Yes, I've been praying for you. Waiting for the moment when I can see you. I think of you a lot sometimes, just randomly as I go about my day. I'm sure about you; I know you are the one for me. I know I can be real with you. I won't fight you or push you if you are not ready to open up to me. I pray my words and demeanor bring you peace of mind, and that you can trust me. I will show you my heart and my actions. Everything is laid out for you. I'm ready for you sweetheart. When I saw you the first time, I knew it was you.

What I Need

What I need from you is more than your physical looks and appearance. Of course, I appreciate that, and value all of your beauty. I need the core of you; I need your essence. I want to feel you wherever I go. I need your peace, your support, love and respect. What I need from you is your youthfulness. Can I joke with you, life is too hard to be stressed. What I need from you is your softness and vulnerability. Can I trust you with what I give? I need your comfort, your wisdom. I take to heart the words that you say to me. What I need from you is your belief as we build and multiply our dreams. What I need from you is your submission. Can you trust the mission I give? I need your words, and support, that you will believe in me even if no one else did. What I need from you is all that you bring. What I need from you is to know yourself and have an understanding of who I am, I need you to know that you are my missing rib.

I Gotta Be

I gotta be the one for you. Not just the man of your dreams, but the man that's gonna pray for you. I gotta be the one for you. That can bring you wisdom and affirm God's word for you. I gotta be the one for you, I gotta be the man that makes you feel safe to be you. I gotta be the one for you. That protects and intercedes for you, I will make your day lighter and bright for you. I gotta be the one for you. I gotta be the one who cherishes your beauty, my love. I hope you feel that I adore you. I gotta be the one for you, that will always feel safe for you, because you are my prize and I value you. I know I am the one for you, that's here to stay and will commitment to you. I gotta be the one for you, to show you my heart has always loved you.

Mask Off

Take off the mask with me, I can see your heart, I can tell you've been hurt. I see all your shortcomings, your flaws and past mistakes. I prayed over it all. It doesn't define who you are, your past is erased.

Please take off the mask, don't hide from me, show me your heart, you are safe. I know all the times you felt alone and afraid in the dark. Disappointed, judged. You got so tired of being used. You tried to mask it all by playing it off, but deep down trying to pretend like you were good, but it wasn't enough. You went further deep in all that stuff, I know it all must have been tough. Listen, you don't have to worry, I got you safe in my arms, so hush. Even if your heart is guarded, I know it's soon to open up, because I'm here with open arms. I am thankful to do life with you. I am happy we are connected. Mask off, just the two of us.

Half Of Me

My guard is down, the veil has been removed. This is me you see, so tell me what you gonna do? Will you accept me for who I am? Not some made-up image in your mind? Do you trust your heart with me? Do you feel like our love is divine? Do you trust yourself not to run from me? Can you tell that this is real? Can you see me in you, like I see myself in you? Can you truly express how you feel? Love is who you are, it calls you by your name. In a blink of an eye, I see the bigger picture; you are only half of me for real. Loving you is loving me, this was already written in God's Will.

Whip Appeal

I can't explain it, but all that you are. You do it for
me.

What do you do to me? It's everything for me.

It gets deeper than words can get; you know how to
get to me.

If I'm not communicating, we still know how to talk.

I like how you appreciate me, you are one with me,
you feel like home to me. Finally, I can breathe. I gaze
in your eyes; I'm drawn in by your essence. I'm fully
tapped into you. I love you girl, you are my greatest
blessing.

Tender

Heart pure of gold

Eyes that see beyond rivers that flow

Young and tender

Laughter and joy in your feet

A life worth living, of abundance of joy and

happiness

You are tender

You're precious in God's sight, all of His thoughts

of you, He looks at you as worthy and His best of

best

You are tender

Sweet never sour, your presence is filled with

warmth. As your spirit lingers, it brings me peace

You are tender, my young and tender

Scriptures

LETTER TO HER

Proverbs 31:11 NIV *"Her husband has full confidence in her and lacks nothing of value.*

Ephesians 5:22-23 NIV *"Wives, submit to your own husbands, as to the Lord. For the husband is the head of the wife even as Christ is the head of the church, his body, and is himself its Savior."*

1 Corinthians 16:14 NIV *"Do everything in love."*

CHAPTER
3

♥

ALL THIS LOVE

Strength

Even in the tears we may cry, we won't lose. There is strength in our love, always trusting that God is on our side. Having full faith and trust in Him will always choose to show up for the sake of love. Saying I will submit and give you every single part of me. Making a conscious decision to say I will comment to His plans and perfect Will concerning me and you. I see strength and God in your eyes every time I look at you. Our life and our family too. I see strength and God every time I look at you.

I Belie e In Lo e

I believe in love

I believe that love exists

I believe in love's connection, that when two people
are drawn towards each other, they will know this is it

I believe in an everlasting love

I believe in true love's first kiss

I believe in a love that will bring forth great pleasure
and the purest joy

I believe in love

I believe love brings much peace

I believe in love, that it will light my soul on fire. A
love so fitting to who I am, that it speaks

I believe in love

I believe in the fruits that love bears. Slow-dancing
into a divinely spiritual heaven bliss

I believe that love is pure gold

I believe in love, that when it finds me, I will feel
safe and at peace. Flowing live into a sea of
refreshing water

I believe in love

I believe in you and me

You know why I believe in love so much?

Because He first loved me

He made me to love

He made me to be. It's His everlasting love that I

experienced, endless encounters in His arms

That's that kind of love God has for you; He has

prepared this love for you and me

His love for you will forever be.

You are always His first love for sure.

Always And Fore er

LOVE – is not just a word you say and take it lightly. Love is a choice. It is a noun and a verb. Love is you and me. We must always choose to LOVE first. Love can be shown through your actions. Show me love and satisfaction. Love is a choice—will you choose to show up for me? Love is understanding. How deep can your love be? Will you vow to love me? And choose love even when I'm not as loving?

Love is a willingness to prioritize my being or happiness above your own.

Love is unconditional affection. Love is sacrifice.

Love is incredibly powerful if it is done the correct way. Love is what God gave to the both of us. Will you surrender your heart for love? I choose to love, always and forever, you and me.

Known

You get me, even the things that I don't often get to speak of. You just get it, you know me, you don't question my ways 'cause you see me. You understand me. You understand my thoughts, my past and have grace for the new me. You embrace me, you look into my future like you already knew me before. I know you get it, because you are me. You're cut from me and that is why you know me. You love me.

Be My Bride

Meet me at the altar in your white dress. Don't just give me only parts of you; I want all of you and everything that's left.

Looking into your heart, I'm searching your thoughts. I want to wash and renew you.
To present you without any blemish, or wrinkle. I want to see the real you.

The real you, who is fearless, and pure at heart. The real you who is free to dance, and worship me with your whole heart.

I will listen to you and answer whenever you call. To reveal my greatest desires for you, I want you to know all my secrets deep within who you are.

Don't you know that I have always been here, chasing after you, searching for you to see me.

I'm ready and available for you, you get to know the real me.

There are parts of me that you haven't even seen; I'm just waiting for you to move so I can tell you what I really mean.

You're my bride and I'm coming, ready and waiting for you. If you hear my voice and harken to my heart, open up, I stand knocking at your door, my beautiful bride you are.

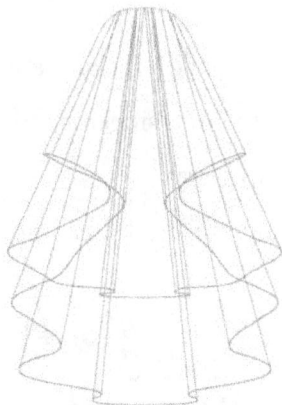

For Me

It's the praise for me, you sing me songs to lift me up.
It's how you pray to me, in a secret place by yourself.
You stay loving me, always wanting me.

The way you worship me, in spirit and in truth. You speak in tongues to me, I send you all my love; you are my joy.

It's your concern for me, you always make sure you include me in your plans. I know you love me and you are down for me.

It's the grace for me, you keep my ground; I'm still standing.

It's your love for me, you make me happy, you bring me joy. You always blessing me, I go from faith to faith, and glory to glory.

Thanks for loving me and for calling me.

Scriptures

<u>ALL THIS LOVE</u>

Colossians 3:14 *NIV "And above all these put on love, which binds everything together in perfect harmony."*

John 15:12 NIV *"This command is this: Love each other as I have loved you.*

1 Corinthian 13:8 NIV *"Love never fails. But where there are prophecies, they will cease; where there are tongues, they will be stilled; where there is knowledge, it will pass away.*

CHAPTER
4

♥

LOVE YOU BETTER

Call

When you call, I will pick up and answer. You are the first person who comes to my mind. When I hear the sound of my text messages go bing, I look down and begin to smile. I've been waiting for you for a while. Can I call you as of now? Will you answer me? "How deep can this love really get?" is what your spirit sings. Let me whisper sweet melodies in your ear. I will comfort you in your time of need if you let me in. You can hide in my secret place, safe and sound; you will find rest. Give me all your worries, your fears, and the pain; I got you covered. Put your trust in me, give me all you got. I'm here listening to you pray as we speak. Call unto me and I will make a sound back. I'm moving beyond the pace of your speed. Yes, it's me. I'm reaching out towards you; you know I got what you need. Wondering like, hmm, if you will answer me back, I'm waiting on your response. Would you say yes? Can you be true? To a person you haven't seen before? Open up to me; don't leave me on read. I'm here calling out to you for sure.

Peace

Peace of mind, peace of thought; yes, you have the peace in my heart. Peace in my laugh, there's peace in my touch, peace in my actions, peace in my ways, peace is the assurance that God has gave. I'm peaceful in the morning, I'm peaceful at night. Peace is our dwelling place, safe in His sight.

It's Unconditional

You keep me, even when I don't feel like being kept. Telling myself I'm gonna open up more to love, I mean, what do I have left? You're patient with me, cutting me with your words, yet gracious in your touch. I feel like I'm floating; I'm breathing through you—it's something I can't explain. I feel full, happy, and at peace. You love me so deeply I can't ignore your presence, all that you are and what you do. Your love for me is unconditional; nothing really has to be explained. As I sit in your love, you see in my heart, you can tell when I'm not being honest or truly myself. You always put me on game. That's why I'm sometimes hard on myself like, why can't I reciprocate the same? The same love, same loyalty, faithfulness, honor and commitment that you give. I feel sad knowing that I will always fall short; I'm not quite sure that you can trust me the same. I know with you I can't walk double-minded; this lukewarm feeling makes me feel like I'm blinded. Yet, again here I am, I still find peace. You speak to me every day, answering my prayers even when I still can't speak. That's gotta be love. Unconditional love and favor you have just for me. What's got into me now? I know I'm not crazy. If I haven't told you before, I'm forever thankful for you. Thank you for being a true friend. I'm down for wherever you take me, and lead me down the path. It's you that works within me, that's why this relationship will always last. You're my best friend, my biggest support system. Because of you, I live, move and have my being.

Honestly

Honestly, I'm tryna stay focused.

Time passing by, how could I have not noticed?

That me being so into myself, I couldn't see you standing next to me. I'm walking to the beat on my own drum, how fast can you catch up with me? No it's not a race, but to be on the same page, you have to catch my rhythm. This part in the beginning, of us talking, has my attention so much because of the feelings, I hope I don't lose me. The feeling of it being hot or cold, you and I both expressing our feelings. Weighting our actions to match our words, honesty is all I've been drilling. Checking to see if I notice a difference in you, the pattern of your ways or it could just be my own toxic thoughts and how I'm feeling. I'm checking myself, honestly, to be open to you has been the greatest feeling. I feel free and happy to take a chance on love. Expressing feelings I haven't felt in a while can be a little overwhelming. I'm honestly praying to God, is this the one for me? It's only been two months since I've been singing,

"Tamia, baby, please be the one." Because each day, I grow to love you more. Extending my grace to you, therefore I can't just tie my feelings to just a thought of a thing. All my endless possibilities and hoping for what love could bring. So I rest and just be. Remembering that I can only be me, me, me. I breathe as I take it slow with you. If you want the whole truth to my heart, ask God to reveal it to you. I'm rooted in him, so in him you will find me, hidden. Honesty, I have nothing to hide about my feelings. Do you? Are you speaking my language? It will be revealed. I'm ready for love now, I can handle it. Honestly, I just thought I'd let you know where I'm coming from and tell you how I feel.

Heal

Heal, I need to heal.

I need a love that's gonna go after me and keep it

real.

Me please heal, I need to heal.

I need a love that can build and keep it real. I need a

love that's not afraid to stay when things get real.

Kinda crazy, kinda funny, I'm just tryna heal.

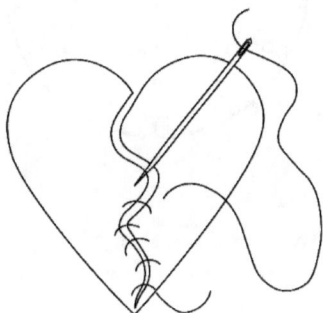

Timing

I know who you are and you know me too.

Waiting on God's appointed time,

what a dream come true.

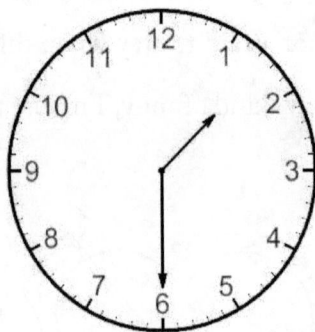

Scriptures

LUV YOU BETTER

Psalm 143:8 NLT *"Let me hear your loving kindness in the morning, for I trust in YOU. teach me the way I should go for I lift up my soul to You."*

Mark 10:9 NIV *"Therefore what God has joined together, let no one separate."*

1 Corinthian 13:4-5 NIV *"Love is patient, love is kind. It does not envy, it does not boast, it is not proud. It does not dishonor others, it is not self-seeking, it is not easily angered, it keeps no record of wrongs."*

Proverbs 3:3-4 NIV *"Let love and faithfulness never leave you; bind them around your neck, write them on the tablet of your heart. Then you will win favor and a good name in the sight of God and man."*

CHAPTER
5

♥

ALL THE THINGS

I'm Thinking

Could it be that I'm for you and you're for me?
Sometimes when I wander off, or go throughout my
day, I think of you. I love you with my heart, I'm sure
you know that it's pure. I love your big warm smile,
your laugh makes me so weak, you bring me so much
joy. I'm excited when I talk to you, even if we don't
have much to say. Can you feel my presence? I don't
know what this could mean for us. It's worth giving
a try, I'm glad we are connected. It's even a breath of
fresh air knowing that we have a strong connection.
Someone so dope like you could exist before I knew
who you were. You just give me a feeling like I knew
you already before. Can you feel me? Are you feeling
what I'm feeling? This is how I feel when I'm with
you, truly. I'm happy I can express my love to you; I
get you and know how you feel.

Lo e

Love on you feels like God.

It's chill, relaxing and very calm with you.

Love on you feels **intentional**.

It's focus, driven, flowing at a steady pace.

Love on you feels pure.

It's being vulnerable and honest with thyself.

Love on you feels passionate.

It's creative, fire, transformative and liberating.

Love on you feels healthy.

It's freeing, clear, and punctual.

Love on you feels peaceful.

It feels gentle and graceful.

Love on you feels whole.

It is rooted, anchored, and secure.

Love on you feels like the glory of God.

LOVE ON YOU.

LOVE ON ME.

The Sweetest Gift

The sweetest gift is waking up to you every day.
To hear the sound of your voice whisper to me I
love you. That's the way love goes.

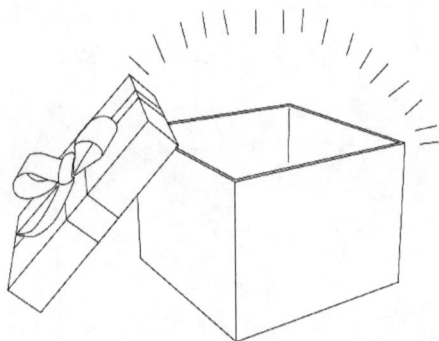

Grace For You

Moments when I want to sink and shut in, I extend my grace for you. Tested with my patience and my love, I make space for you. I open myself up so you can see my heart; my love goes out for you. How long will you hide it from me? Open up your heart, I'm trying to be real with you. To show you this love you must be willing, willing to dance into the midnight hours, late night walks and talks with you. Can I tell you a secret, something that really turns me on? Honesty gets me wet, it's my biggest foreplay and truth with you.

My Greatest Inspiration

You take me higher, like a stream of river that flows, your love sets me on fire. Passion in your eyes, with a spirit full of grace. Each night I breathe you, taking in all your thoughts like they're mine. You are divine, one of a kind, I can't even lie. You take me higher, to another level that I never knew existed. Yes, I will meet you there, I'm digging all your ways, I'm taking all of you, I will fully commit.

You motivate me to do better, I want to live right and have this life abundantly with you. You inspire my very beginning; you push me further into purpose.

I'm feeling the way you touch my soul; your words make my spirit jump. You hold a light in me, in every part of me.

You always see the best in me.

You are wonderful, created in God's image, you are a powerful human being. The best gift that God has ever given me. I'm thankful to have you, and to experience all that you are. You're my favorite, and greatest, my favorite and greatest inspiration.

Self-Lo e

Self-love. You probably get asked this a lot, what's it to you? People think that self-love is about getting money, shopping bags, going places—you know, the luxury things. Yet, there's more to self-love than we think'. The self-love we claim we want is really God's love, and some people still don't have a clue. Self-love was originally created to showcase God's love just for you. It gets deep once you've unveiled your deepest dark lies, something like the ugly truth. Nights of real tears, the real you, the vulnerable you, the one who always feels attached to pain, people, money, or maybe even fame. The self-love that's more in tune with finding you. The self-love that restores my spirit from its broken frame. The self-love that can only show hidden secrets of you and sweet whispers of love notes into the night. You see, self-love is the best love; it's what we truly long for each day. The self-love that gives you peace of mind as you go about your day. Get this self-love and I pray you will be gentle this time to yourself. Self-love is not found in women or men, nor even material things. This self-love is found in you alone. Love yourself always.

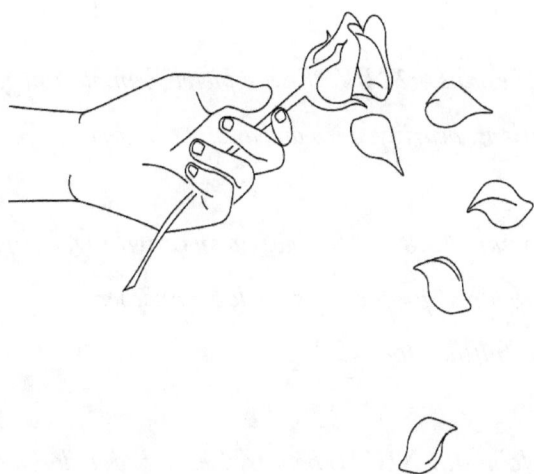

Scriptures

ALL THE THINGS

1 Peter 4:8 NLT "Most of all, have true love for each other. Love covers many sins."

Ephesians 4:2 NIV "Be completely humble and gentle; be patient, bearing with one another in love."

Romans 13:8 NLT "Owe no one anything, except to love each other, for the one who loves another has fulfilled the law."

1 John 4:8 NIV "Whoever does not love does not know God, because God is love."

CHAPTER
6

♥

OU KNOW WHAT'S UP

Mindful Beha ior

Mindful behavior. Let's play a game of concentrate. Feel yourself deeply rooted in Him. I think that would make a perfect date. Your body is pure, a holy temple, I'm waiting to explore.

I feel closer to God with you, maybe that's why I feel who you are. I can finally just be. Your rhyme challenges me to pick up the pace. I feel you. You never say words that don't align with your actions. That's love at its best. Keep it simple. I like that about you, I can rest. Show me something new, I'm in the right place at the right time, I know it's you. I believe in you. May I ask? What do you have in store for me? Focus, all I want to do is concentrate on you. Can I demonstrate my love for you? I'll let my body explain if you want me to. Yea, I can go there with you. Tapping into your wounded scars, allow me to heal you. Release all your frustrations on me, allow me to feed you through my worship, as I submit my mind, body and devotion to you. Can we concentrate and go deeper, digging into the mind of you. I want to climax in your thoughts and unravel the thoughts that don't belong. I get you, I'm learning and growing by understanding who you are. I'm focused now, more diligent, consistent to you. Let's focus, no more games. I know I'm divinely in tune with you.

Commune With You

Let's make an agreement, let's go to a place where we both can sit and just talk freely, to let go of our past thoughts, all the places that we once fought. Places where we fought so hard to fit in, to get along with others, just to make time pass. Can we truly see the beauty in our differences? A love so perfect by God it was made to last? Let's be clear, how are you feeling? Can we both open up? Exploring the possibilities of this thing called love. That can truly help. Love is real, love is God and it's in you and me. You get it now, I can see clearly into you, so let's just be. I hear you, even when I don't have much to say. I have discerned your being and movements; I feel your thoughts, even the ones you don't even get a chance to say. Why is that? 'Cause I truly know how you feel. Let's agree to always come to this place of love for each other, and always keep it real.

I Want That

I want that, "I can't wait until you get home" kinda love, "I'm sending you messages from my heart that reads you" kinda love. The kinda love that makes people stop and ask, "have you seen the way that he looks at her?" kinda love. I want the kinda love that's so real and almost too good to be true kinda love. The kinda love that makes my spirit jump, you understand what I feel kinda love. I want that good love, "I'm yearning for ya, everyday" kinda love. I want that kinda love that gets you high, just because, kinda love. I want that "wherever you go, I will go" kinda love. The kinda love that's less talk and more action kinda love. I want that love that stands true to the end of time and is affirming, kinda love.

I want that kinda love that makes me smile whenever I hear your voice kinda love. I want that "come here, let me tell you something" kinda love. I want that.

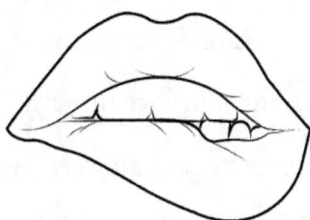

Rain Down

Rain down on me

Heal me with your love

Your tender kisses on the back of my neck

Holding me tight in your arms, let's go get wet as

we rub

Back to back, body to body

Rain down on me

Pour out your love into my heart

Sweet morning texts and flowers just because, see deeply into me. I want to feel you; shower me with all your innermost thoughts. I bathe you, come closer, into me as we go higher, I'm talking infinite, as you take a taste of my thoughts and my being. Come into me and see what I mean and what I'm saying. You speak my language and answer me with reassurance that you support my truth. We're naked, body to body, you were made divinely, sent from heaven, the spotlight is yours. Rain down on me, from start to finish, you are the truth.

What Turns You On?

What turns your love on for me?

If it pleases you, can I talk to you?

I want to just sit.

Can I be in your presence, engulfed in your love?

I wanna rock with you all night.

Whisper words to mend your heart.

What turns me on?

I love when you sing to me.

What Is Lo e?

Sitting here thinking about our conversations like wow! Amazed at how well things flow between us. Everything seems to come naturally with you. It's easy and I mean that in a good way. Nothing seems complicated with you, it's organic. Bringing forth peace, love, and the purest abundance of joy of them all. I can run to you, I feel safe with you, and I like that above all.

Scriptures

YOU KNOW WHAT'S UP

Song of Songs 8-6 NLT " *Place me like a seal over your heart, like a seal on your arm. For love is as strong as death, its jealousy as enduring as the grave. Love flashes like fire, the brightest kind of flame.*

Song of Songs 8-7 NLT " *Many waters cannot quench love, nor can rivers drown it. If a man tried to buy love with all his wealth, his offer would be utterly scorned.*

Romans 12:10 NIV " *Be devoted to one another in love. Honor one another above yourself".*

1 John 4:18 NIV " *There is no fear in love. But perfect love drives out fear, because fear has to do with punishment. The one who fears is not made perfect in love."*

www.ingramcontent.com/pod-product-compliance
Lightning Source LLC
LaVergne TN
LVHW051813080426
835513LV00017B/1936